How many college ... to change a light b...

Only one, but he gets 37 college credits for it.

* * *

What's the difference between a hockey player and a pit bull terrier?

Skates.

* * *

A guy walked into a bar that was a hangout for professional athletes. The place was pretty empty. He was on his second drink when he spotted a tall, rugged-looking guy sitting morosely in the corner, crying into his beer. The guy gestured to the bartender and asked, "What's with that guy over there?"

The bartender said, "He's had three no-hitters in a row."

The guy exclaimed, "Then why isn't he celebrating?"

"Because he's a boxer," the bartender replied.

THE JOCK JOKE BOOK

THE JOCK JOKE BOOK

EWELL WINCE

PaperJacks LTD.

TORONTO   NEW YORK

AN ORIGINAL

PaperJacks

THE JOCK JOKE BOOK

PaperJacks LTD.

330 STEELCASE RD. E., MARKHAM, ONT. L3R 2M1
210 FIFTH AVE., NEW YORK, N.Y. 10010

First edition published April 1988

ISBN 0-7701-0810-5

THE JOCK JOKE BOOK

TABLE OF CONTENTS

Section One: Baseball Jokes 1

Section Two: Football Jokes 27

Section Three: Basketball Jokes 57

Section Four: Tennis Jokes 67

Section Five: Golf Jokes 73

Section Six: Hockey Jokes 81

Section Seven: Boxing Jokes 87

Section Eight: Jokes About Other Sports 93

Baseball Jokes

St. Peter stood at the pearly gates, questioning the latest arrivals who sought admittance to heaven. He asked the first guy in line, "What was your favorite baseball team?"

"The Yankees," the guy replied.

"Sorry," St. Peter said. "No good. Take the elevator to the depths below."

The dejected sinner walked away while St. Peter asked a second man about his favorite team.

"The Baltimore Orioles," the man replied. St. Peter shook his head and pointed toward the elevator.

The next guy in line, a rather timid soul, started to turn away also. St. Peter grabbed his arm and said, "You have to be questioned. What was your favorite team?"

The guy grimaced. "For sixty years, I followed the Chicago Cubs."

St. Peter beamed. "Welcome to heaven," he said. "As a Cub fan, you've had your hell on earth."

* * *

A black baseball star, accompanied by two advertising execs, was flying over the Rockies in a small jet on his way to make a commercial on the West Coast. The pilot, a staunch Southerner, had made the trip highly unpleasant with his racist remarks. Suddenly, however, the pilot's attention was directed elsewhere as an engine caught fire. The pilot got the plane under control, but it began to lose altitude. The pilot turned to the passengers and said, "We got to shed some weight. One person is going to have to jump to save the rest of us. It can't be me, because I have to fly the plane. So I'll ask the rest of you questions, and the first guy to miss a question has to jump."

"Wait a minute," the baseball player said. "That's not fair. I know what you think of blacks."

The pilot thought for a second, then said, "I'll make it fair. All the questions will be about baseball."

"Fair enough," the black guy said.

The pilot turned to the first corporate exec and asked, "Who won the 1986 World Series?"

"That's easy. The Mets."

"Right," the pilot said. He turned to the second exec and asked, "How many people attended the last game of the series?"

The guy thought hard, then said, "About 50,000."

"Right," the pilot said. Then he turned to the black baseball player and said, "Name them."

* * *

Mario Vespucci came to the United States from Italy as a boy and worked hard all his life to support his wife and seven sons. One boy became a doctor, two became lawyers, and three had good jobs in business. But Mario's proudest day came when his youngest son Joseph signed a contract with the New York Mets. He was so happy that he arranged for his 90-year-old father to fly over from Italy to see young Joe play his first game at Shea Stadium.

The elder Vespucci was still a vigorous man, and he sat upright in his box seat as the game started. Mario started to explain the rules of the game in Italian when the first Met batter, Mookie Wilson, drilled a pitch to left center. "Run, Mookie, Run!" screamed the crowd. A moment later the ninety-year-old Italian man joined them. The next two batters struck out, but when Gary Carter doubled down the line, the old Italian got to his feet to yella, "Runna, Gary, Runna."

Finally, in the bottom of the second, young Joe Vespucci finally made his appearance at the plate. Then Vespucci saw the umpire signal ball one, ball two, ball three, and finally ball four. Joe tossed his bat away, and started to walk to first base.

"Runna, Joe, runna," the old man screamed.

"No, Poppa," Mario told his father. "You don't understand. He got four balls, so he walks."

A huge glow lit the old Italian's face. He shook his fist and screamed, "Walk tall, my Joey, walk tall!"

* * *

What's the difference between a baseball groupie and a moped?

They're both fun to ride until your friends see you.

* * *

What's an ugly baseball groupie?

A girl who sleeps with the trainer.

* * *

Why are there more baseball groupies than ever this year?

They heard the players talking about how much more lively their balls were this year.

* * *

What did one bird say to the other as they were flying over Wrigley Field?

"Let's put everything we've got on the Cubs."

* * *

What's the most prevalent condition that afflicts baseball groupies?

Athlete's fetus.

* * *

Since they knew he couldn't get a job anywhere else, the team made the ex-catcher a coach and assigned him to keep track of all the equipment during batting practice. He was doing his job one day when a vicious line drive clocked the third baseman on the head, knocking him out.

As another coach ran to help, he yelled to the ex-catcher, "Run in the clubhouse and tell the manager."

The ex-catcher did as he was told. He knocked on the manager's door and said, "Uh, skipper, one of the guys got beaned bad by a ball during practice."

The manager leaped to his feet. "Which one?"

The ex-catcher shrugged. "I dunno. All them balls look alike."

* * *

The star pitcher wined and dined the beautiful blonde he met after the ball game. He managed to talk her into coming back to his hotel room, where he took her in his arms and whispered, "Darling, I fell madly in love with you the moment I saw you. I don't think I'll be able to live without you always at my side."

"Now, now, wait a minute," the blonde said, pulling away. "We've just met. I'm not sure I want to get serious."

The pitcher shrugged. "So who's serious?"

Why did all the New York Yankee wives have their husbands tested for AIDS?

To make sure they'd be safe at home.

* * *

Why did the baseball groupie only go for players over 6' 6" tall?

She was a sucker for a high hard one.

* * *

Why are most major-league baseball players so comfortable at singles bars?

They've spent a lot of time in the bush leagues.

* * *

Why do some women only date shortstops?

Shortstops position themselves deep in the hole.

* * *

Milly was in her early sixties now, but she was fond of regaling her friends with racy stories about all the famous athletes she'd slept with. Her friends dismissed the stories as wishful thinking until Milly took them along to an Old Timers' Day game at Yankee Stadium. After the former ballplayers participated in a three-inning exhibition, Milly led her friends to a spot under the stadium. To their amazement, the old women could peek through a hole into the shower of the men's locker room. The only problem was that one peephole gave a view of the players from the waist down and one peephole gave a view only from the waist up.

Milly took the lower hole. She peered in and said, "Oh, my goodness. There's Joe DiMaggio on the left. Then

Duke Snider is next to him. And Willie Mays is all the way to the right.''

Her friend looking through the upper hole stepped back in amazement and exclaimed, ''Why she's right! How do you know who's who?''

Milly winked. ''I told you. I must know half the members of the Baseball Hall of Fame.''

* * *

What's a jockstrap?
   A ball-bearing device.

* * *

Two baseball groupies were sitting at the bar after the game when the team began filing in. One pointed to a tall outfielder and said, ''Boy, that guy is really hung!''

''Yeah,'' her friend agreed. ''You've said a mouthful.''

* * *

Two fans were leaving the stadium club well after a game when they spotted some movement in the players' parking lot. They wandered over and saw a young girl fondling the genitals of a well-known third baseman.

''What do you know?'' one guy said to the other. ''We've got a Yankee and a yanker.''

* * *

The pitcher for the White Sox finally got married, and after much urging, agreed to take his new bride on a road trip. The team plane arrived in Baltimore and took a bus to the hotel. The pitcher and his wife were on the elevator heading up to their room when a gorgeous young blonde in a mini-miniskirt got on the elevator. When she saw the pitcher, she grinned and cooed, "Why, Georgie darling, back in town so soon?"

The pitcher nodded his head nervously while his wife glared at him. When they got to their room, she exploded. "Tell me who the hell that was!" she demanded.

"Honey," the pitcher said, "don't get on my case. I'm going to have a tough enough time explaining you to her."

* * *

Did you hear about the new chastity belt for baseball groupies?

A catcher's mask.

* * *

How does a baseball manager know he's in first place?

When fans wave at him, they use more than one finger.

* * *

Did you hear that the Los Angeles Dodgers finally hired a black baseball scout?

His territory is the Bermuda Triangle.

* * *

What do a Mafia Godfather and Pete Rose have in common?

Four thousand hits.

* * *

The all-star outfielder was doubled up in pain in front of his locker an hour before the first game of the World Series. His manager, desperate to get the outfielder back on his feet, put in an immediate call to the team physician.

* * *

The physician and the manager carried the outfielder into the trainer's room. The physician said, "Tell me, what's wrong?"

"It's my cock," the outfielder groaned. The physician helped him pull down his pants and, sure enough, the guy's cock was swollen to the size of a football.

"Goddammit," the manager swore. "You've been screwing around with those groupies again. Didn't I warn you to take precautions?"

"Cap, I did take precautions," the player groaned.

"What precautions?" the physician asked.

"I gave every single one of those bitches a phony name and address."

* * *

What's the difference between your wife and the Chicago Cubs?

Year in and year out, the Cubs still suck.

* * *

The baseball pitcher was coming on to the woman at the bar. She grimaced and said, "You jocks are all alike — you've got your brains in your dick."

The pitcher grinned. "Then how about blowing my mind?"

* * *

Why didn't the baseball slugger ever marry?

He heard marriage produces a hitch in your swinging.

* * *

The young major-league pitcher had just signed a whopping new contract, and to celebrate he flew in his relatives from the hills of West Virginia. Since many of them had never even worn shoes, the pitcher figured that New York would dazzle them, but a day-long sightseeing tour produced only a few polite grunts. Finally, that evening, he rented a limousine for the trip to Yankee Stadium. On the way he told them, ''Tonight you'll see why the Yankees are paying me $1 million a year.''

An hour later, the pitcher was on the mound. The first batter up lined a single to left. The next guy doubled. Before the pitcher knew it, seven consecutive batters had reached base and he was on his way to the showers.

He expected to find his relatives depressed at his failure, but instead, they were in the stands grinning and whooping it up. ''Gosh, dang, cousin,'' one guy said to him. ''You sure did find yourself the easiest way to make a million bucks we ever did hear about!''

* * *

The baseball player had gotten married in the off season, and in the locker room on opening day, he told reporters that he was soon to become a father.

''When are you expecting?'' a reporter asked.

''Any day now,'' the player replied. ''She's just entered the top of the ninth.''

* * *

The youngster showed up at the stadium for his new job as bat boy. One player thought he'd rib the kid. He winked at the other guys, then asked, ''Bring me a male bat, son.''

To his surprise, the kid just nodded, went off, then returned with a bat.

To save face, the player demanded, ''Son, can you tell me exactly how you tell a male bat from a female bat?''

The boy looked at him with a grin. ''I can tell by the way they're stacked.''

* * *

Why did the baseball player know his marriage was in trouble?

He was traded from the Yankees to the Dodgers and discovered he still had the same milkman.

* * *

Did you hear that Dodger Stadium has the classiest locker rooms in the big leagues?

Even the steam room is air-conditioned.

* * *

The manager called a player's wife in and said, "All this talk about divorce at home is really upsetting your husband. I don't think you'd find a better man. He's so consistent as a ballplayer, the same performance week in and week out."

The wife grimaced. "That's the problem. He's consistent in bed, too — weak in and weak out."

* * *

Two guys were out for a good time, so the cabbie said, "I'll take you to this really neat whorehouse. The madam's an ex-baseball groupie."

The two guys said that sounded okay, and the cabbie dropped them off. They walked inside. To their surprise, the living room looked just like a major-league dugout. The madam came up to them and asked, "You two want to play ball today?"

The guys said they did. So the madam gave them a tour. They walked into another room where several beautiful girls were doing exercises. "This is the bullpen," the madam explained. Next came the locker room, where the guys undressed. Finally, they came into a smaller room where five naked guys sat on the floor pulling at their dicks.

"What do you call this?" one guy asked the madam.

"Don't you know anything about baseball?" the madam snapped. "This is the on-deck circle jerk."

Did you hear about the gay baseball manager?

He cornered a rookie in the shower room to show him how he could make it big in the majors.

* * *

What happens when a nymphomaniac gets on the team bus?

Everyone gets off.

* * *

One baseball player was sitting in the locker room when a friend came over and asked, "Hey, Fred, you still seeing that gorgeous blonde you met after the game last month?"

"Nah," Fred replied. "She was really stacked. But she was too dumb."

"What do you mean, dumb?" his friend asked.

"Well, I told her I loved her."

"So what does that have to do with being dumb?"

"She believed me," the player replied.

* * *

After all the hoopla about discrimination in baseball, the new manager of the Dodgers hired a black man as one of his three new coaches. He called the men into his office, then said to one of the white guys, "George, you coach the hitters during batting practice and coach first base during the games."

George nodded.

The manager turned to the second white man and said, "Rube, you coach the pitchers during warmup and coach third base during the games."

Rube nodded.

The black man couldn't restrain himself. He asked, "Skipper, what's my job?"

The manager turned to him and said, "You're the sex and music coach."

The black coach was puzzled. "The sex and music coach?"

"Yeah," the manager replied. "If I want your fucking advice, I'll whistle."

* * *

What do baseball announcers say when a black hitter steps to the plate?

"The Jig is up."

* * *

What's long and hard and red and comes with balls?

A sequoia baseball bat.

* * *

Why did the Polack keep coming back to the Yankee Stadium box office to buy another ticket?

The guy at the gate kept tearing his in half.

* * *

A Polish guy took the afternoon off to go to a ball game. An hour later his boss was surprised to see him coming into work. "What happened?" the boss asked.

"I had a lousy seat," the Polack replied. "I'm so short, and this guy in front of me was so tall, I couldn't see a thing."

"So why didn't you change seats with somebody?" the boss asked.

"I couldn't. There wasn't another person sitting any-where near us."

* * *

A Polack was sitting with his girlfriend in Wrigley Field when a pigeon flew overhead and dumped his load right on her. The girl turned to her boyfriend and said, "Go to the men's room and get me some toilet paper."

The Polack replied, "Why bother? That bird's a mile away by now."

* * *

What's the toughest part about managing a black pitcher?
Sending him to the showers.

* * *

What's the first thing a major-league baseball player does every morning?
He gets up and drives back to the team hotel.

* * *

What's a George Steinbrenner sandwich?
One that's so full of baloney you can't swallow it.

* * *

The baseball player was still in bed when the room-service waiter arrived with breakfast. The waiter put the tray on the table. Noticing the female garments strewn all over the room and hearing the sound of a female voice singing in the shower, the waiter asked the player, "Anything for your wife, sir?"

The player thought a moment, then said, "Yeah, I guess so. Go down to the gift shop and get me a couple of postcards."

* * *

Why did they call Dwight Gooden an overachiever?
Nearly every day, he'd reach a new high.

* * *

The baseball player was talking with the blonde at the bar when she asked seductively, "Do you cheat on your wife?"
He shrugged, "Who else would I cheat on?"

* * *

The pitcher showed up in the dugout with a monstrous hangover, and the manager chewed him out royally. He ended up shouting, "All this whoring around isn't fair to your wife. What would you say if she allowed herself to be picked up in a bar?"
The pitcher replied, "Finders, keepers."

* * *

Why did the kid get cut from the baseball team?
His father'd always told him that the key to success was striking out on your own.

* * *

Why does Don Mattingly make $2 million dollars a year?
A good batter makes good dough.

* * *

A guy came a little late to his buddy's house to watch the World Series. He walked in the room and asked, "How's it going?"
"Third down, and 21 to go."
"Wait a second," the guy said. "Are you watching football?"

"I wasn't talking about the game," the friend said. "I'm talking about this case of beer."

* * *

What's the difference between a religious revival meeting and a baseball game?

At a religious revival, they shout, "Stand up for Jesus," and at a baseball game they yell, "Sit down, for Christ's sake!"

* * *

Why is playing baseball exactly like dating a Jewish American Princess?

Before you start, you've got to have a diamond.

* * *

Why do ballplayers smoke marijuana?

They like to spend their afternoons and their evenings on grass.

* * *

At the neighborhood barbeque, the couples were sitting around the table when one guy said to the group, "Hey, did you hear about the guy who tried to trade his wife for a season's tickets to the Mets games?"

"That's disgusting!" one woman remarked. She turned to her husband and said, "Fred wouldn't do anything like that, would you, dear?"

"Absolutely not," her husband replied. "The season's half over."

* * *

The phone rang in the hotel room of the star pitcher. The gorgeous young blonde who was sharing his bed picked up the receiver and said, "Hello."

"What in the fuck are you doing there?" the team manager shouted. "I need that guy at the stadium right now. He's the ace of my staff."

"I'm sorry," the girl replied sweetly, "but right now I've got your ace in my hole."

* * *

The rookie asked his manager, "Is it all right to have sex before I pitch?"

The manager replied, "As long as you don't do it on the mound."

* * *

If nine black men and a monkey started a baseball team, what position would the monkey play?

He'd be the manager.

* * *

Why do blacks love baseball?

Because they can shake a stick at whitey and get away with it.

* * *

Jesse Jackson called the baseball commissioner and demanded, "We want any player, manager, coach, or umpire that uses the word 'nigger' to be permanently banned from the game."

The commissioner said, "Jesse, be reasonable. We can't ban bad language. Why, the word 'bastard' is used ten times as much as the word 'nigger.'"

Reverend Jackson replied, "Well you bastards aren't as well organized as we niggers."

Two guys were sitting in a bar in the Bronx, and one was griping about his job. "All I do for eight or ten or twelve hours a day is sit in that bathroom in Yankee Stadium and wait for George Steinbrenner to come in."

"You're a rest-room attendent?" the other guy asked.

"Worse. I have to unzip the boss's pants, help him sit down, then wipe his ass afterward. And if I don't do a perfect job, he yells at me and docks my pay."

"That's demeaning," the other guy said. "Why don't you quit?"

The first guy grew indignant. "Quit? And leave professional baseball at my young age?"

* * *

The outfielder was home from a long road trip, and after sex, his wife cuddled up to him and asked, "So, did you miss me?"

The ballplayer didn't seem to notice, so his wife asked, "Jack, is there anything wrong? You seem preoccupied."

Jack sighed and replied, "No, it's not you."

"Are things going badly on the field?"

Jack said, "No, I'm hitting .323, my best season."

"Then what's wrong?"

Jack replied, "Well, if you insist on knowing... when I left my girlfriend in the maternity ward of that St. Louis hospital, she had the nerve to accuse me of not caring about her or the baby."

* * *

The Yankee third baseman was home from a long road trip, so the manager was surprised to see him lingering in the clubhouse for another beer after the rest of the players had departed. The manager went up to him and asked, "Sonny, why aren't you home with your wife?"

The infielder replied, "When I got home, I found out she'd run away with my best friend."

"God, I can't believe she left you. That guy must have been really good-looking!"

Sonny shrugged. "I can't say. I never met the guy."

* * *

The years had put a big belly on the team manager, but his wife was proud of how she'd kept her weight. The two sat at a table, watching the young ballplayers talk up the beautiful groupies sitting at the bar. The wife turned to the husband and said, "You know, I'm so proud of myself. I can still get into the same skirts I could get into when I was 25."

The grizzled manager stared at the huge tits on a gorgeous young blonde and grunted, "I wish I could say the same."

* * *

The baseball player brought the blonde back to his hotel room. While they were undressing, she noticed the little box attached to the bed. "What's this for?" she asked.

The player replied, "If you put a quarter in, the bed starts vibrating. I'll find a quarter and..."

The blonde stopped him, saying, "Don't worry, sugar. When you get a quarter in, I start vibrating."

* * *

Did you hear about the new line of men's underwear called Umpire?

It signals you when your balls are foul.

* * *

What do major-league pitchers and gigolos have in common?

Fast balls.

* * *

What do Polish women having their period have in common with a Boston sports team?
   They both have red socks.

* * *

Why is virginity like a no-hit game?
   Just one time at bat can end it.

* * *

Did you hear about the ugly baseball player?
   When he was born, the doctor slapped his mother instead.

* * *

What do you get when you cross a baseball groupie and a pitcher's prick?
   Sticky lips.

* * *

Why don't gay baseball players lean on their bats?
   They don't want to risk getting serious on the field.

* * *

Why is George Steinbrenner like a diaper?
   He's always on somebody's ass, and he's usually full of shit.

* * *

What do you call it when you get VD from a baseball player?
   Athlete's cunt.

* * *

Why is sex like baseball?
  The quality depends on who's at bat.

* * *

Why didn't the baseball groupie ever get pregnant?
  She blew all her chances.

* * *

What did the groupie do when she broke into the Yankee locker room?
  She kissed everyone in the joint.

* * *

Why did the leper get kicked off the baseball team?
  He dropped a ball in left field.

* * *

Why did the leper go blind playing baseball?
  He kept his eyes on the ball.

* * *

The catcher was so ugly that he was the one guy on the team that had trouble getting women. But one day he came into the locker room with a huge grin on his face. He took the trainer aside and said, "Look, Sal, you gotta help me. I met these two Swedish stewardesses last night, and I talked them into coming over to my place tonight. You gotta get that black bag of yours and give me something that will get me up and keep me up and pumping away all night."
  The trainer agreed. He took the catcher into his

office and gave him a pill from a special personal supply. He cautioned, "This stuff is powerful. I'd only take half a pill if I were you."

The catcher thanked him and was the first one out of the locker room. The next day, he was the last player at the stadium, and he walked in looking like death warmed over. He staggered to the trainer's room and pleaded, "Please, Sal, get out the Ben●Gay."

The trainer said, "You can't put Ben●Gay on your dick— you'll go through the roof."

The catcher sighed, "It's not for my dick, it's for my elbow—I took the whole pill, but those fucking broads never showed up."

* * *

The baseball groupie went back to the hotel with the outfielder. The moment they climbed into the sack, she pushed him over on his back and climbed aboard.

"What are you doing?" the player asked.

"You play for the Cubs, right?" she asked.

"So?"

"So the Cubs always fuck up," she replied.

* * *

Why did the leper pitcher retire?

He threw his arm out.

* * *

Three gays were discussing their favorite sports. "I love football!" the first fag explained. "I love all those beautiful buns and those tight jerseys."

"You silly!" the second queer said. "I love boxing. All

those big muscles covered with sweat right out for me to see.''

The third gay stood and said, ''You don't know what you're talking about. I like baseball. I can imagine being up at the plate with the bases loaded in a crowded stadium. The pitcher throws strike one, but the bat's on my shoulder. The pitcher throws strike two, and the bat stays on my shoulder.''

''What's so great about that?'' one of the other fags asked.

''Recognition, darling,'' the third queer says. ''Before the pitcher winds up again, 50,000 fans shout, 'Swing the bat, you cocksucker!'''

* * *

What do baseball players do when they come across a beautiful groupie?

Wipe it off.

* * *

Why do the best-looking baseball groupies stay away from rookies?

They wait until they've got some experience under their belts.

* * *

The runner on first took off on a steal attempt and slid headfirst toward the bag. The second baseman leaped into the air to take the throw, then came down with all his weight on the runner's hand, mangling it with his spikes.

The runner passed out, then woke up in the hospital the next day. He saw a doctor above him and asked, ''Doc, how am I?''

The doctor said, ''Well, I've got some good news and some bad news.''

''Gimme the bad news first.''

The doctor said, "We had to amputate your left hand. You'll never play again."

"Oh, no!" the player exclaimed. "What could possibly be the good news?"

"The guy they signed on to replace you wants to buy your glove."

* * *

Did you hear about the Mississippi town that couldn't decide between starting a chapter of the Ku Klux Klan and organizing a baseball league?

They compromised by hunting down blacks and beating them to death with bats.

* * *

Why do baseball owners love the idea of having female players?

They wouldn't have to pay them one-tenth as much.

* * *

A baseball star entered one of his hangouts to find a beautiful and extremely well-built blonde girl he'd dated before sitting in a booth, weeping over a brandy. He sat down opposite her and asked, "Julie, what's wrong?"

"Everything," she sobbed. "My parents were killed in an automobile accident last week, I was fired from my job, I'm being evicted from my apartment, and I discovered I have terminal cancer."

"That's terrible," he said consolingly. "What about if I take you out Saturday night and cheer you up?"

She shook her head no. "I've decided to kill myself Saturday night."

He shrugged and said, "Well, what about Friday night?"

Did you hear about the baseball player who found it easy to get to first base with his female fans?

He was finally thrown out at home.

* * *

An institution for the mentally retarded arranged for its inmates to attend a baseball game. The director spent days training his charges to obey his commands so there wouldn't be any trouble.

The day of the game was bright and sunny, and the group arrived just before the first pitch. When it was time for the national anthem, the director yelled, "Up, nuts!" and the inmates immediately rose. When the national anthem was over, the director yelled, "Down, nuts!" and the inmates sat.

The game proceeded, and the inmates were well behaved. When the home team made a good play, the director yelled, "Clap, nuts," and they applauded just like the other fans. In fact, things were going so well that the director left his seat to go get a hot dog and a beer. But when he came back, there was a riot going on. The director finally located his assistant and demanded, "What happened?"

"Everything was fine," the assistant said, "until some guy came over and yelled, 'Peanuts!'"

* * *

Fred was taking his son Joey to the ball game for the first time, and he wanted to make sure the kid had a good time. Before they went to their seats, Fred stopped at the refreshment stand and bought the kid two hot dogs with mustard and sauerkraut, french fries, and a large Coke.

In the first inning, Joey turned to his dad and started to say, "Daddy, I want..."

Fred interrupted, "I know, you want popcorn." He motioned the vender over and bought a large bag.

The next inning, Joey said, "Daddy, I want..."

Fred stopped him again and bought cotton candy.

The third inning, Joey said, "Daddy, I really want..."

"It's ice cream," Fred said. He bought a big cup.

The next inning, Joey turned to Fred and vomited noisily into his lap.

"What in the hell did you do that for?" the father demanded.

Joey replied, "Since the first inning, I've been trying to tell you I want to throw up."

* * *

Football Jokes

The fire was raging through the apartment building, and a huge crowd had gathered as a mother appeared in a seventh-floor window, holding her three-month-old baby. The mother screamed for help, but the ladder on the fire truck was too short to reach.

The situation looked hopeless until a tall, slender black man pushed his way through the crowd and said to the fire chief, "Hey, man, you know me? I'm Ace Dawkins, the all-star wide receiver for the Colts."

The chief said, "Yeah, I've seen you play. But I can't talk now—we've got a baby to save."

"That's why I'm here," the receiver said. "I've got the best hands in the world. Tell that mother to drop the baby, and I'll guarantee I'll catch him."

The chief thought for a moment, then realized there was no other choice. He got a bullhorn and told the mother what the plan was. She hesitated, but with the flames licking at her back, she agreed.

Dawkins got ready. The mother kissed the baby, then

dropped it seventy feet. A gust of wind caught the infant, but the wide receiver dove to his left, caught the baby in his arms, then hit the sidewalk and rolled so perfectly that the baby was never even jarred.

The black held the baby up in the air triumphantly as the crowd went wild. Then, with a big grin, he spiked the baby on the sidewalk.

* * *

The Alabama quarterback was easily the most arrogant football player reporters had ever met. He looked like a Greek god and he considered himself the most perfect person ever put on the face of the earth. Just before the start of practice for his senior year, he walked into the office of the team doctor for his required physical. He said to the doctor, "Doc, this is a waste of your time. Just sign my form—my fans are waiting outside."

The doctor bristled at the egomaniac, then said, "I'm paid to examine you, and I'm going to do it. You never know, I might find something."

"No way," the quarterback replied. "I'll make you a bet—if you find something wrong with me, I'll give you two season's tickets on the 50-yard line. But when you find that I'm in perfect shape, you'll have to give me twenty minutes alone in here with that gorgeous nurse of yours."

"It's a bet," the doctor said. He then proceeded with an incredibly thorough examination. To his regret, however, he could find nothing wrong. The grin on the quarterback's face got wider and wider until the doctor said, "It's time to check inside. Bend over."

The quarterback bent over the table, and the doctor inserted a finger deep in his rectum. The quarterback grimaced slightly, then stood up and said, "So bring in that nurse."

"One more test," the doctor said. "Open your mouth again." When the quarterback complied, the doctor shoved his shit-covered finger down his throat. The quarterback turned green, then vomited all over the office.

"Ah, just as I suspected," the doctor said. "Stomach problems."

* * *

Why do college football linemen have cracks between their toes?
   So they can carry their library cards.

* * *

What did the football lineman do when he broke his toe?
   Called a tow truck.

* * *

How can you tell if a football player has been raiding your refrigerator?
   From the handprints in the butter.

* * *

What do you get when you cross a defensive lineman with a prostitute?
   A quarter-ton pickup.

* * *

What do you find between Refrigerator Perry's toes?
   Slow running backs.

* * *

St. Peter was stationed at the pearly gates when he was

surprised to see the star black running back from the University of Mississippi standing in front of him.

"What are you doing here?" St. Peter asked.

"What's wrong, man?" the dude replied. "Don't you allow no black folks in here?"

"Only those with special qualifications," St. Peter said.

"Well, I made first team all-American my sophomore year," the black replied.

St. Peter looked unimpressed.

"I set a national record for most yards rushing as a junior."

St. Peter still didn't budge.

The football player tried a third time. "My senior year, I was the first black at Ole Miss to marry a white cheerleader."

"Really?" St. Peter asked, suddenly interested. "When was that?"

"About five minutes ago," the black man replied.

* * *

The football coach was leaving the gym when he saw one of his big linemen lumbering toward him, chasing a young kid. He managed to stop the giant player, demanding, "What in the hell do you think you're doing?"

The angry lineman said, "Coach, I caught the kid stealing the laces out of one of my shoes."

"So?" the coach replied.

"So the little bastard wouldn't even tell me which shoe."

* * *

A manufacturing company received an order from the psychology department of the university for two dozen huge wire cages measuring seven feet high by six feet wide. The president thought the order must be a clerical error, so he called the chairman of the psychology department.

"No," the chairman replied, "the order is correct. Those

cages are for two dozen football players we're using for an experiment."

"Football players?" the manufacturer replied in astonishment. "I thought you did all your experiments on rats?"

"We used to," the psychologist replied, "but we got so attached to the rats.

* * *

A sign was posted on the science building bulletin board: "Wanted — male student to participate in research project. Compensation up to $500. Sign up in biology department office."

A huge line immediately formed, but the students dispersed quickly when they found out exactly what the research project entailed. A half hour later, the only person outside the door was a burly tackle from the football team. The chairman of the biology department invited him to sit down, then explained, "We're recruiting a participant for a study in cross-breeding between human beings and primates. In plainer words, your job would be to have sex with a female gorilla. Are you interested?"

"Great!" the lineman said. Then a frown crossed his face.

"Is there a problem?" the professor asked.

"Well," the lineman replied, "there is one thing. Is it okay if I pay you the $500 in installments when I get my meal money every month?"

* *

A strange-looking man in a filthy black trench coat walked into a supermarket and went to the produce department. He told the clerk he wanted to buy half of a head of lettuce. The clerk told him he couldn't sell him half a head. Without a word, the strange man whipped a huge sword from under his coat, raised it over his head, and viciously slashed a head of lettuce in half. Then he picked up the half and went to the front of the store.

The cashier didn't know what to charge the guy, so he asked him to wait while he checked with the manager. He went into the office and said to the manager, "Some crazy asshole out front wants to buy half a head of lettuce."

At that moment, the cashier happened to look around and saw the strange man raising the sword over his head. Quickly, he said to the manager, "And this nice gentleman has agreed to buy the other half."

The next day, the manager called the cashier into his office and said, "Son, I was impressed by your quick thinking yesterday. I called the home office and got you a scholarship to take a management training course at the University of Oklahoma."

"I appreciate it, sir," the young man said. "But I wish it wasn't Oklahoma. The only people they turn out are football players and nymphomaniacs."

The manager's face turned red with anger. "My daughter attends the University of Oklahoma."

"Oh," the cashier said. "What position does she play?"

* * *

The playboy quarterback for the Jets found the usual crowd of autograph seekers outside the stadium after the victory. He spent about twenty minutes obliging all the requests and finally came to the last man in line, a tough-looking guy in his twenties. The handsome football star reached for the expected pen and paper, but instead he found a pistol shoved into his gut.

"Hey," the quarterback protested. "What's your problem? If you want money, my wallet's..."

"No money," the man said. "I want you to beat off, right here in the parking lot."

"No way," the quarterback said. "You're..." His voice

trailed off when he heard the pistol being cocked. He unzipped his pants and did as the guy asked.

When he was finished, he asked, "Can I go now?"

"Do it again," the man demanded.

Before the Jets star could protest, he found the gun at his temple. He beat off a second time, then a third time, then, with the gun in his mouth, he managed a fourth effort.

Spent, he collapsed to his knees. "Please," he begged. "No more. Shoot me."

The guy put his gun away. "I'm not gonna shoot you." He turned and called out into the darkness, "Sis, you can come up and meet the guy now."

* * *

Did you hear about the football lineman whose coach told him to put on a clean jock every day?

By the sixth day, he couldn't get his pants on over them.

* * *

Did you hear about the football coach who was fired for being gay?

They found out he'd drilled every member of the team.

* * *

The young draftee went out on the town after practice with three Steeler veterans. They walked into a bar and had a few drinks. As the young football player loosened up, he confided to the veterans that he'd never had much luck with women.

One of the veterans slapped him on the back and said, "Boy, that was before you joined the Steelers. Women here will do anything for the team."

"Anything?" the kid asked.

"We'll show you. Come on." He followed them over to a

well-built young blonde sitting in the corner. One of the veterans whispered in her ear. She got up and followed them into a back room.

One of the veterans said, "Now, watch this, kid." He turned to the girl and barked, "First down." She immediately unzipped his pants and gave him a blow job.

The second veteran stepped up and said, "Second down." He got the same treatment. The third veteran yelled, "Third down," and he got his reward.

The kid could hardly restrain himself. The minute the third veteran shot his load, the kid unzipped his pants, jumped forward, and shouted, "Fourth down!" The girl turned to him and kicked him viciously in the balls.

The kid slumped to the floor, writhing in pain. A few minutes later, when he got his breath, he turned to one of the veterans and whispered, "What happened?"

"Don't you know shit about football, boy?" the veteran snapped. "Even that nympho over there knows you're supposed to punt on fourth down."

* * *

Bruno the tackle came back to the dorm one night and excitedly told his friend Joe, the quarterback, "Hey, I got engaged tonight."

"To whom?" Joe asked.

"Glenda. The cheerleader."

The quarterback shook his head, "Jesus, Bruno, you don't want to marry her. She's fucked every guy on the team, offense and defense."

Bruno thought for a moment, then shook his head. "Gee, that is a lot of guys," he replied. He slowly walked away.

Two weeks later, Joe ran into Bruno again in the dorm. "Hey, Joe, I got engaged!" Bruno exclaimed.

Joe winced. "You mean, you're still going to marry that nympho Glenda?"

"Nah, I ditched her. I'm engaged to Wilma West."

"The basketball cheerleader? Jesus, Bruno, she's fucked every guy on the basketball team."

Bruno grinned. "I know. But that's only five guys."

* * *

It was love at first sight for Linda and Bob, who met on the first day of their freshman year at Yale. It turned out they were both superior students fascinated by great literature. By the middle of their senior year, they were both headed toward graduating summa cum laude. Immediately after graduation, they planned to marry.

Then tragedy struck. While Bob was driving back to school from Christmas vacation, his car skidded on an icy pavement and crashed into a telephone pole. Linda rushed to the hospital, where the doctors told her, "We can't control the bleeding from his head injuries. The only way we can save his life is to remove 90 percent of his brain. He won't be the same person, but..."

Linda collapsed, weeping. By the time Bob came out of surgery, she'd pulled herself together enough to go in to visit the shell of the man she loved. But to her shock, Bob had disappeared from the hospital.

Months turned into years, with still no word of Bob. Linda assumed he was dead until a friend called her years later and said, "Linda, I saw Bob on TV yesterday."

Linda exclaimed, "That's impossible."

"No, it was Bob."

Linda said, "You've got to be mistaken. They removed 90 percent of his brain. What could he possibly be doing?"

The friend replied, "The guy on television said he was head football coach at the University of Oklahoma."

* * *

The college football star was being interviewed for the first time on national television. The announcer asked, "Jocko, where are you from?"

"I'm from Nebraska, sir," the linebacker replied.

"What part?" the announcer asked.

"All of me," Jocko replied.

* * *

The athletic director at Southern Cal came to the university's chancellor to show him a newspaper report charging that the new football coach had punched out a player at spring practice. The two men called the coach on the carpet. The coach's face turned red with anger. He stood, pointed at the chancellor, and screamed, "I do my job the way I want to do it. Just take that paper and shit on it." He turned to the athletic director and added, "And as for you, you faggot, you can go back to your office and fuck yourself in the ass."

With that the coach stormed out. The chancellor took a deep breath, then asked the athletic director, "Just how good is that jerk?"

The athletic director said, "He's won eight conference championships and seven bowl games in the last ten years."

The chancellor thought for a second, then stood up. "Well, that settles it," he said as he started to unzip his pants, "I guess I'm taking this newspaper with me into the john. But I'm afraid you've got a very serious sex problem."

* * *

Why did the dumb football lineman trot out onto the field with his pants off?

He was told it was an exhibition game.

* * *

A couple of pro football players were sitting at the bar talking about a certain quarterback in the league. "I don't understand how that guy's got time to play football. All he's got on his mind is cunt, cunt, cunt.''

"How do you know all he has is cunt on the brain?" the other guy asked.

"Well, once a month he gets a nosebleed."

* * *

Did you hear that Refrigerator Perry's got sex organs in his feet?

If he steps on you, you're screwed.

* * *

What's long and hard for a football lineman?

The second grade.

* * *

What's the difference between big tits and the Columbia University football team?

There's nobody in the world who doesn't look forward to playing them.

* * *

What do the ''NFL Today'' and a Nebraska cheerleader's thigh have in common?

They're both pigskin previews.

* * *

Why do black football players wear helmets?

If they didn't, their heads would stick to the Astro turf.

* * *

Two football linemen walked into a bar after a road game

and ordered a couple beers. To their annoyance, they spotted a decidedly effeminate chap sipping white wine a few stools away.

"Hey," one player yelled to the bartender, "what kind of place is this? What's that fairy doing here?"

The bartender shrugged. "He's minding his own business."

The lineman growled, "I'll take care of this." He walked over to the fag and said, "Get the fuck out of here."

"Wait a minute," the gay chap replied. "I'll make you a bet. If I beat you at a game of bar football, I get to stay."

"You can't beat me at nothing," the lineman sneered. "Go ahead, show me what this bar football is."

The fag ordered a pitcher of beer. When it arrived, he chugged it all without taking a breath, then yelled, "Touchdown." A moment later, he dropped his pants, let out a huge fart, and shouted, "Extra point. 7-0."

The lineman grinned and said, "I can do that." He ordered a pitcher of beer, downed it in a flash, then yelled, "Touchdown. 7-6." Then he dropped his pants and bent over.

But before he could fart the fag jumped foreward, rammed his prick up the lineman's ass, and screamed, "Block that kick!"

* * *

What do you get when you bury 50,000 blacks up to their necks in a football stadium?

Afro-Turf.

* * *

The coach at the rural agricultural college inherited the dumbest group of football players he'd ever seen. He finally got them sorted out into offense and defense. Then he realized he needed a punter. He picked out one of the smaller guys, took him off to the side, and said, "I want you to practice punting."

"What's punting?" the guy asked.

"Punting is when you hold a ball in your hands, drop it, then kick it."

"How do I know when to punt?" the genius asked.

"I'll give you the signal," the coach said. "When I nod my head, you kick it. Understand?"

The player said he did. The coach nodded his head. Then player kicked. The coach lost five teeth.

* * *

The football coach at the agricultural school was so desperate for players that he put up signs all over the school announcing tryouts. To his astonishment, a large turkey waddled out onto the field the next day. The coach tried to kick him off the field, but the turkey said, "Listen. At least give me a chance."

The coach agreed, and put the turkey in at quarterback. On the first play, the gobbler grabbed the ball with one wing and heaved a 40-yard pass. On the next play, he ran a quarterback sweep for another 25 yards. On the third play, he bootlegged around left end for a touchdown.

The coach was ecstatic. He went up to the turkey and said, "You made the team. If you play for a full season, I'll give you a four-year scholarship."

"Forget the scholarship," the turkey said. "All I have to know is, does that full season last until after Thanskgiving?"

* * *

The new defensive back from the hick college went out drinking with the defensive linemen one night. The next morning he showed up at practice with a couple of black eyes and a swollen lip. The coach asked, "What happened?"

"Gee, Coach," the guy said, "we was in the bar having a couple drinks, when I started to tell O'Reilly a joke about the pope."

"Boy, that's stupid," the coach said. "Didn't you know O'Reilly was Catholic?"

"Yeah," the defensive back said, "but how in the hell could I know the pope was?"

* * *

What's the best way to keep your husband from watching football all day Sunday?

Shoot him on Saturday night.

* * *

A young boy wandered into the den where his father was watching the Giants play the Redskins. His father asked him if he wanted to watch, saying, "Maybe you'll be a pro football player some day."

"I can't," the boy replied.

"Why not?"

"Because those players aren't real people — they're all robots."

"That's foolish," the father said. "How do you know they're mechanical men."

"They must be," they boy replied. "When you were out of town last week, I heard Mom telling Mrs. Smith how she met a guy on the team and screwed his ass off."

* * *

How can you tell a lineman from a running back at a pro football team's training table?

Running backs peel bananas before they eat them.

* * *

Did you hear about the Polish football team?

They were on the other team's two-yard line, and the quarterback faded back to throw a sixty-yard pass.

The quarterback looked like a Greek god, tall, blond, and handsome. He had very little trouble persuading the gorgeous Hollywood starlet to come back to his hotel room. When he undressed, however, the starlet noticed that his cock was barely two inches long.

"I can't believe it," she said. "Just who do you expect to please with that little thing?"

The quarterback grinned. "Me."

* * *

The football player walked into the training room to be taped and sat down. The trainer noticed he was scratching his head like crazy, and asked, "Rocco, what's wrong?"

"My head itches," the lineman replied. "I got this dandruff."

"I can tell you what to do for that," the trainer said. "You just go out and get some Head & Shoulders."

"Gee, thanks," Rocco said.

A few days later, the lineman came back into the trainer's room, still scratching his head. "Didn't you follow my advice?" the trainer asked.

"I tried to," Rocco said. "The head was great. But my girlfriend didn't know how to do shoulders."

* * *

Why do football players like women with big tits and small pussies?

Because football players have big mouths and small dicks.

* * *

Did you hear about the University of Nebraska lineman who won the pie-eating contest?

The cow sat on him.

* * *

Why is a dance chaperone like a football defensive back?
   They both spend most of their time intercepting passes.

* * *

What's football?
   A sport in which it takes a fan four quarters to finish a fifth.

* * *

How can you tell your wife's getting fed up with "Monday Night Football"?
   When she strips, comes in the den, stands in front of the TV set, and announces, "Play me or trade me."

* * *

Giant Stadium was packed for a key late-season game with the Redskins. That's why the empty seat was so noticeable. When the beer vendor was called over by the guy in the seat next to the empty one, he asked, "Say, how come that seat's empty?"
   The guy replied, "That's my wife's seat."
   The vendor said, "Where is she?"
   "She's dead."
   "I'm sorry," the vendor said. He gave the guy his beer and his change, then said, "Couldn't you find a friend or relative to use that ticket?"
   "Nah," the guy said. "They're all at her funeral."

* * *

How does a Texas high school football coach sort his players by position?
   He sends his squad sprinting toward a brick wall. Those who go through it are linemen, those who run around it are backs.

Doris's husband was so obsessed by football that their sex life was nonexistent. Desperate, she consulted her best friend, who said, "Why don't you just dump the guy?"

"I can't," Doris said. "I love him. Besides, he's a good husband the rest of the year. I wouldn't even mind the football if I didn't need to get laid."

"Then here's what you do," the friend said. "On Monday night, I'll watch your kids over here. You completely undress, then watch the game on another set. When the gun sounds for half time, you walk sexily into the den. It's got to work."

Doris thought it was a terrific idea. But Monday night, she showed up at her friend's house in tears. "What happened?" the friend asked.

"I thought it was working," she moaned. "Then suddenly he sent me to the kitchen."

"Why?"

"The replays came on," Doris wailed. "He wanted to watch, so he gave me fifteen yards for illegal use of hands."

* * *

Why was the Polish punter kicked off the team?

Every time the center snapped the ball, he called a fair catch.

* * *

Why do so many college coeds date football players?

Football players are always really stiff after a game.

* * *

Why is being an heiress like being a pro football return specialist?

In both cases, you have to wait for somebody to kick off before you receive.

* * *

How tough is professional football?

Well, on the first day of Dallas Cowboy practice, there were two broken legs, a concussion, a fractured rib, and an eye injury — and that just covers the Cowgirls.

* * *

Why does the University of Nebraska have artificial turf in its stadium?

To keep the cheerleaders from grazing at half time.

* * *

Penn State was down by two touchdowns when the coach turned to a giant lineman and said, "Stankowski, get in the game and kick some ass!"

"Right, Coach," Stankowski said. "What's his number?"

* * *

Did you know the state of Texas has only three official sports?

High school football, college football, and professional football.

* * *

What's fe-fi-fo-fi-fo?

The snap count in a Harlem football game.

* * *

Time had to be called in the college football game when one of the cheerleaders was discovered leading some yells from the 40-yard line. The angry coach marched over to her and snapped, "Young lady, you're way out of position. Have you had your eyes checked recently?"

The sweet little thing cooed, "Why, no, Coach, they've always been blue."

* * *

The new coach was being interviewed by the Notre Dame Alumni Association. After reviewing his impressive credentials, the head of the alumni group said, "Coach, with six national championships at two different schools, you're obviously the best man for the job. We know you've got a big job ahead of you here turning around this program, and you've got all the time you need. We're behind you 100 percent, whether you win — or win big."

* * *

Did you hear about the flash flood at the football stadium?

After 80,000 fans had been drinking beer for three quarters, the cheerleaders got up and shouted, "Go! Go! Go!"

* * *

The star quarterback was showing the prospective recruit around campus. They walked into the cafeteria at the student center and the quarterback began pointing out celebrities. He gestured toward a gigantic guy wearing a letter sweater and said, "That's Cibulski, our all-American defensive end." He turned and nodded toward an athletic-looking black guy wearing a letter sweater and commented, "Jefferson broke the conference record for rushing as a sophomore." The quarterback was about to lead the prospect out of the cafeteria when the high school senior stopped him, then pointed to a very short, thin, nerdy-looking guy in thick glasses who also wore a letter sweater covered with stars. "I don't believe it," the prospect said. "What's that guy doing wearing a letter sweater?"

The quarterback replied, "That's Herman Smith. He's

the most important person in the entire football program.''

''You're kidding? What's his position?''

The quarterback said, ''He takes all of our tests.''

* * *

The Alabama Crimson Tide football program was under fire for the racist attitudes of its coaches. A reporter from a TV network went down to the school to investigate.

The head coach allowed the reporter to listen in on a prepractice speech. In the speech, the coach told his team, ''There's no such thing as race on the football field. All that matters is competing for the pride and glory of the Crimson Tide. On the field, we're not black or white, but warriors in red.''

The reporter was very impressed. He followed the team as it went out onto the practice field. Then he heard the coach bark, ''All right, I want all of you light red guys over here, and all of you dark red guys over by the tackling dummies.''

* * *

After the football team was trounced 54-0 on national television, an obnoxious TV reporter stopped the losing coach and asked, ''What do you think of your team's execution?''

The coach growled, ''I think it's a damn good idea.''

* * *

What's a football coach?

A loud, hard-driving, aggressive man whose father was a bachelor.

* * *

Jefferson was 6' 2", 210 pounds, and he looked as athletic as any of the other blacks trying out for the University of Mississippi football team. But he finished an amazing dead last in the 40-yard dash, behind even the big white linemen.

After the race, the coach came over to him and said, "Boy, turn in your uniform."

Jefferson pleaded for another chance. After nearly an hour of begging, the coach gave in and let him take his turn with the quarterbacks. On the first snap, Jefferson faded back and threw a perfect 80-yard touchdown pass. As the coach watched in awe, Jefferson then completed 19 of the next 20 passes he threw.

After the display, the coach told him, "All right, boy, you can be my quarterback. But I'll tell you right now, you got to listen to what I say. Folks around here ain't gonna like having a nigger quarterback, and if you fuck up, the Klan will have you hanging from a tree. Understand?"

Jefferson agreed. A month later, Ole Miss started the season against number-one-ranked Alabama. To the delight of the coach and fans, Jefferson had a great game. With one second left, Ole Miss led by four points. The coach sent in a player to tell Jefferson to run a quarterback sneak to run out the clock.

But when the black quarterback got to the line of scrimmage, he saw all eleven Alabama players on the line of scrimmage and he couldn't help himself. He changed the play, took the snap, faded back, and released a 50-yard pass. However, Alabama's star defensive back, who was an Olympic sprinter, used his great speed to get back to intercept. The sprinter wove his way through the Ole Miss team and headed toward the end zone. To the intense dismay of the Ole Miss coach, the only player near him was Jefferson, and he was ten yards behind.

Unable to watch, the coach turned his back. When he heard the crowd roar, he said to his assistant, "Tell me the bad news."

The assistant coach screamed, "Coach, we won. Jefferson tackled him on the two-yard line."

The coach was stunned. He ran out to Jefferson and asked, "How in the hell did you catch that guy? You're slower than my grandmother!"

Jefferson replied, "Coach, that guy be running for a touchdown. I be running for my life."

* * *

What's the best way to beat up a football lineman?

Slam the toilet lid down on his head when he's taking a drink.

* * *

Why is the NFL going to use a green football next year?

You ever hear of a black dropping a watermelon?

* * *

Why are Tony Dorsett and Walter Payton like jockstraps?

They're all professional ball carriers.

* * *

How did the University of Alabama repave their stadium parking lot?

They called a rally of black students, then ran a steamroller over them.

* * *

What's the title of the new black assistant football coach at Ole Miss?

"Boy."

* * *

The star quarterback was invited to talk to the Booster Club meeting about the subject of sex and the professional athlete. However, he was afraid his wife wouldn't understand, so he told her the subject of the lecture was sailing.

A week after the speech, his wife ran into a man who'd been at the meeting. The guy mentioned how terrific the quarterback's speech had been.

"I don't understand," the wife said. "He knows so little about the subject."

"Oh, come on," the guy said. "He obviously knew what he was talking about."

"But he's only tried it twice," the wife protested. "The first time he lost his hat and the second time he got violently seasick."

* * *

What's a "fuck-off?"
The selection process for the Dallas Cowboy cheerleaders.

* * *

Two good old Southern boys were sitting in front of the gas station drinking some beers when one said to the other, "Hey, you hear a couple of those nigger players up at the university are wanted for raping some of those young coeds?"

The other guy shook his head. "What's this world comin' to? Those niggers are getting all the good jobs."

* * *

The Chicago Bears' defensive tackle walked into the barroom and announced to the regulars, "I'm the biggest, baddest, maddest, meanest black dude in the entire NFL. I make half a million dollars a year, I drive a Rolls-Royce, I drink the finest whiskey, and I only fuck white women. Now who wants to buy me a drink?"

A guy at the end of the bar waved him over and ordered

a fine single malt Scotch. The lineman chatted with the man for few minutes while he finished the whiskey, then announced, "I'm the biggest, baddest, maddest, meanest black dude in the entire NFL. I make half a million dollars a year, I drive a Rolls-Royce, I drink the finest whiskey, and I only fuck white women. Now, who wants to buy me a drink?" A second sitting at the table bought the lineman a drink and got his few minutes of conversation.

After the lineman gave his speech a third time, a skinny guy at the bar waved him over. But after a few seconds of conversation, the lineman picked the guy up by the collar and threw him over the bar. The guy smashed into the wall, then fell unconscious to the floor as the lineman stalked out.

Five minutes later the guy came to. The other patrons asked what had happened. The guy grimaced and said, "I don't know. All I said to him was, if I made a half million dollars a year, I wouldn't fuck niggers either."

* * *

The football lineman was sitting in English class when the professor called on him. "Mr. Cibulski, have you read the assigned Shakespeare?"

"Can't say I have," the lineman replied. "Who wrote it?"

* * *

What do football players like better than a cold Budweiser?
   A warm Busch.

* * *

What do the Arkansas cheerleaders use as douche?
   Hog wash.

* * *

The doctor finished his preseason examination of the football lineman. Then he asked the big question. "Tell me," he said, "have you ever had a problem with steroids?"

"No, sir," the lineman replied. "Not since I started using Preparation H."

* * *

The football lineman was the last to shower and the last to get dressed. Then he decided he had to go to the bathroom. A couple of minutes later he shouted to the team trainer, "Hey, there's no toilet paper in here!"

"We're all out," the trainer yelled.

"What should I do?"

"Got your wallet?" the trainer asked.

"Yeah," the player replied.

"Well, use a dollar."

There was silence. Then an angry lineman stormed out of the bathroom with his hand covered with shit. "Stupid advice," he snarled. "I'm still covered with shit and now I've got four quarters stuck up my ass."

* * *

Why do Jews play football?
   They love to get the quarter back.

* * *

Why did they call timeout at the leper football game?
   There was a hand off at the line of scrimmage.

* * *

Why did the leper football player go back in the shower?
   He forgot his head and shoulders.

* * *

Why do blacks make such good wide receivers?
Colored folks was always good at fetching.

* * *

What's the difference between Refrigerator Perry and an African hippo?
A hippo's five pounds lighter and doesn't eat chicken.

* * *

Did you hear about the new all-gay NFL squad?
They're the perfect come-from-behind team.

* * *

What's the difference between an Ethiopian baby and an NFL football?
An NFL football has to weigh at least 14 ounces.

* * *

Why are college football players like astronauts?
They both take up space in school.

* * *

How do they teach linemen to put on their uniform pants the right way?
"Brown in back, yellow in front."

* * *

Why did the New York Giants draft two gays and a hooker?
They needed two tight ends and a wide receiver.

* * *

Why don't lepers play quarterback?
One hard pass rush, and they go to pieces.

* * *

Who teaches cheerleaders about oral sex?
The head coach.

* * *

What's the difference between a football lineman and an Italian grandmother?
A black dress.

* * *

What's black and white and red all over?
The Oakland Raider team bus after it's been smashed by a speeding semi.

* * *

What's the Harlem High School football cheer?
"Barbeque, watermelon,
Cadillac car
We're not as dumb
As you think we be!"

* * *

The college coach was fired after his team lost the first five games, and an assistant was promoted to the top job. Lost about what to do, he talked to a friend who coached at a school that had already walloped his team.

"What's wrong with us?" he asked the other school's coach.

"It's your execution," the friend replied. "You can see

from the press box that half your team screws up on every play. Either your guys are too dumb or your plays are too complicated. In either case, I'd throw out your playbook and put in some real simple stuff.''

The new coach thought that was good advice. He called his squad together and told them, ''Boys, we're only going to have four plays in our entire playbook — NRR, NRL, SPDN, and WBK.''

The star running back looked puzzled. ''What be NRR, Coach?''

''NRR,'' explained the coach, ''stands for Nigger Run Right. NRL means Nigger Run Left. SPDN means Same Play, Different Nigger. And WBK means White Boy Kick.''

* * *

The football lineman walked into the Penn State pizzeria and ordered a pie.

''Do you want that cut into four or eight slices?'' the counterman asked him.

''Four,'' the lineman replied. ''I can't eat eight slices.''

* * *

Why doesn't the Nebraska football team have ice water on the bench?

The player with the recipe graduated.

* * *

Why is it so dangerous to have black cheerleaders in stadiums with Astro turf?

When they do splits, they stick to the floor.

* * *

How did Refrigerator Perry know he was overweight?
   He stepped on his dog's tail and it died.

What's more macho than playing tackle football naked?
   Playing flag football naked.

* * *

Why did the dumb girl refuse to date football players?
   She heard that none of their balls were round.

* * *

Why are so many wide receivers gay?
   They're obsessed with getting into the end zone.

* * *

How did the girl land the wide receiver as a date?
   She had a great fly pattern.

* * *

Why do cheerleaders wear such sexy outfits?
   They make the fan's root harder.

* * *

Why is the United States Football League like a sixty-five-year-old whore?
   They both got fucked for $3.00

* * *

Did you hear the NFL Players Association has agreed to voluntary drug testing?
They agreed to test any drug they were given.

* * *

How does a girl get to be a Dallas Cowboy cheerleader?
She just has to make the team.

* * *

What happened to the girl who laid the entire football team?
She was named an honorary wide receiver.

Basketball Jokes

The black basketball star was low-bridged on a dunk shot and he hit the floor hard, breaking his leg in two places. Still in uniform, he was rushed to the hospital. The emergency room nurse started to prep him for surgery, when she noticed the head of his penis sticking out the leg of his basketball shorts. She was so amazed that she couldn't help but start laughing.

The basketball star glared at her angrily. "You can laugh, bitch, but if your old man broke his leg, his prick would shrink, too."

* * *

How did his teammates know Len Bias was addicted to cocaine?

Every time the whistle blew, he'd start sniffing the foul line.

* * *

Why did the rooster go to the basketball game?
He heard two referees were blowing fouls.

* * *

What would you get if you slipped amphetamines to Bobby Knight?
A prick that stayed up all night.

* * *

Did you hear about the black basketball star who negotiated his own million-dollar contract without an agent?
He got a dollar a year for a million years.

* * *

Did you hear about the black college basketball star who wrote to tell his mother he'd grown another foot?
She sent him a sock.

* * *

What's the definition of eternity?
The length of time before a white man wins the NBA Slam Dunk Competition.

* * *

Why did Pepsi-Cola sue the NBA Players Association?
Because their new slogan was, "Coke is it."

* * *

Why do most pro basketball teams take two or three live monkeys on road trips?
In case someone gets hurt, they've got spare parts.

What's Mayor Ed Koch's new plan to stop mugging and rapes in Harlem?

He's giving away 100,000 free basketballs.

* * *

What's the most important coaching tool for a Harlem basketball coach?

A wheelbarrow. It teaches the kids to walk on their hind legs.

* * *

Did you hear that Ronald Reagan just created 12,000 new jobs for blacks?

He added 1,000 teams to the NBA.

* * *

Did you hear about the college basketball star who got his diploma in just three terms?

Nixon's, Carter's, and Reagan's.

* * *

Why are so many young black basketball stars unable to get college scholarships?

They can jump, they can run, they can shoot, but they can't pass.

* * *

Everybody was astounded when the 7' 4" center showed up for the team party with a tiny 4' 10" woman he introduced as his fiancée. Later, a buddy took him aside and said, ''I've got to ask you. You weigh five times as much as she does. How in the hell can you make love?''

"It's easy," the big guy said. "I sit in a chair, hold her in front of me, and move her up and down on my lap. It's as easy as beating off, only I got someone to talk to."

* * *

Why do so many proctologists go to Indiana University basketball games?

Because they've heard that when He made Bobby Knight, God created the perfect asshole.

* * *

Why did the basketball star's wife insist that he not have knee surgery?

She was afraid it would make him limp.

* * *

Why do black basketball players have such prominent posteriors?

When God made the first black dude, he granted him one wish. The black dude replied, "I wants to get my ass high."

* * *

Why do black kids wear basketball shoes?

It keeps them from biting their nails.

* * *

Two North Carolina State basketball players were holding a press conference to refute charges that the school's athletes paid little attention to their schoolwork.

"This investigation is a lot of jive," one player said. "The guys on the team all make As and Bs."

"That's right, bro," the other player said. "And we be working on the rest of that alphabet right now."

The black assistant coach was hired to recruit in the inner city. After a few days on the road, he showed up with a gigantic seven-foot center who could shoot, rebound, pass, and block shots. The head coach was really impressed, but he had doubts about the giant's formal education.

"He's okay," the assistant coach said.

"I'll give him a test," the head coach said. He turned to the huge dude and asked, "Can you tell me how much 8 and 8 is?"

The giant thought for a second, then said, "8 and 8 be 11."

The assistant coach stepped in with a smile and said, "See, Coach, I told you he wasn't dumb — he only missed by three."

* * *

What's basketball?

It's a sport where ten superb black athletes in perfect physical condition run up and down a court in front of 15,000 white spectators who could use the exercise.

* * *

Why are basketball groupies like alcoholics?

They both love highballs.

* * *

What do you call a basketball team riding in a bus?

A blood vessel.

* * *

What do you call a hooker sucking off a black basketball player?

A blood transfusion.

What do a basketball game and a gay bar have in common?
  All you see is swish, swish, swish.

* * *

How many college basketball players does it take to change a light bulb?
  Only one, but he gets 37 college credits for it.

* * *

What do black basketball players use for jock itch?
  Black Flag.

* * *

Why aren't there any women playing in the NBA?
  Every time one walks into the locker room, she gets blackballed.

* * *

  The white sportswriter was at the urinal in the locker room when the big black center came racing in, whipped out his huge cock, started to pee, and sighed, "Boy, I just made it."
  The sportswriter pointed to the big dick and asked, "Can you make me one, too?"

* * *

Why did the entire leper basketball team end up in wheelchairs?
  They were de-feeted in their first game.

* * *

How do we know Jesus was a good rebounder?

He really got up high on the boards.

* * *

Three young nuns from the convent were out in the yard shooting a few baskets when Monsignor Reilly walked by. The priest had been quite a player in his youth, and after watching for a moment, he asked the sisters if he could join them for a game of two on two.

Monsignor Reilly took the ball, faked, drove the lane like a pro, but blew an easy lay-up. The priest's face turned red and he exclaimed, "Jesus fucking Christ, I missed!"

The sisters almost keeled over from shock. They glanced in horror at each other but kept silent.

The other team scored, then Monsignor Reilly got the ball again. He tried a jump shot, but the ball spun around the rim and kicked out. "Jesus fucking Christ, I missed!" the priest roared again.

This time one of the sisters said, "Monsignor, please. God will strike you down right here if you don't stop taking the holy name of His son in vain."

The game went on for a few minutes. With the score tied and one basket needed to win, the monsignor posted up a shorter nun, took a pass, faked left, then spun for a short hook shot. The ball missed the rim completely, then fell off the boards into the hands of a nun from the other team, who put in a lay-up for the victory.

The monsignor was furious. *"Jesus fucking Christ, I missed!"* he shouted. Suddenly, the skies darkened, a deafening clap of thunder echoed, then a bolt of lightning shot out of the sky and fried one of the three nuns.

A couple of seconds later, a voice boomed from the heavens, "Jesus fucking Christ, I missed!"

* * *

The two basketball coaches were on a scouting trip to Harlem. One coach was grousing to the other about the filthy, crowded streets. "I hate this part of the job. All these loud, dumb fucking niggers crowding the streets."

They crossed a street on their way to a high school gym, when they spotted an organ grinder on the corner. His monkey was doing incredible acrobatics, leaping straight up in the air five feet, doing flips, tossing a ball from hand to hand. The first coach watched for a moment, then went over and dropped a $10 bill into the organ grinder's cup.

"What are you doing?" the other coach asked. "I thought you hated these street niggers."

"I do," came the reply. "But that guy's little kid looks like he could grow up to be a player."

* * *

What's the definition of worthless?
A 7′ 4″ black with a small cock who can't play basketball.

* * *

What do you get when you cross a black and a groundhog?
Six more weeks of basketball season.

* * *

Why are all black basketball players so tall?
If a black is less than 6′ 2″, his knuckles scrape the floor.

* * *

Why did the big black basketball star rent a tuxedo and a chauffeured limousine to take him to his vasectomy?
If he was gonna be impotent, he wanted to look impotent.

* * *

The black high school basketball star received a four-year scholarship to Harvard, but some of the very snobbish upperclassmen didn't like the idea of lowering social and academic standards to improve the performance of the prestigious school's athletic teams. A group of the snobs were walking across campus one day when the black freshman stopped them and asked, "Can you dudes tell me where the science building is at?"

The snobs snickered. One said haughtily, "You should know that at Harvard, we do not end our sentences with prepositions."

"All right," the black dude replied. "Can you tell me where the science building is at, motherfuckers?"

* * *

What's the definition of the word "renege"?
  Substituting five new players on the basketball court.

* * *

Why did the black basketball player throw away his headband?
  It wouldn't play a damn bit of music.

* * *

What do you get when you cross a 6' 10" black basketball star and a 5' 4" white groupie?
  An abortion.

* * *

What do you call a pro basketball player who turns down free cocaine?
  Dead.

* * *

What do pro basketball players do when they're accused of using drugs?
    Hire a crack attorney.

* * *

Why did the Boston Celtics think Len Bias was like a wildflower?
    Two days after they picked him, he died.

* * *

How do you make the Len Bias All-Star Basketball Team?
    You have to be six feet and under.

* * *

Where's Len Bias playing basketball now?
    I don't know, but it must be stiff competition.

* * *

What's black on the outside and white on the inside?
    An NBA player's nose.

* * *

What kind of basketball do they play in Hawaii?
    Hula hoops.

* * *

Why are blacks so good at basketball and rape?
    They both involve jamming balls into holes.

Tennis Jokes

Why didn't Martina Navratilova play in the Dutch Open?
  She got her finger stuck in a dyke.

* * *

Why does Martina Navratilova have the cleanest cunt in tennis?
  She has a colored maid come twice a week.

* * *

What do lesbians like better than Calvin Kleins?
  Billy Jeans.

* * *

Why is Billy Jean King so good at tennis?
  She swings both ways.

* * *

How do we know that Martina Navratilova is popular on the women's tennis circuit?

Because all the women eat her up and no man is down on her.

* * *

What has fuzzy balls and eats pussy?

Martina Navratilova.

* * *

What does Martina Navratilova do when her opponent makes a mistake?

Gives her a tongue-lashing.

* * *

Does Martina Navratilova like to cook?

No, she prefers eating out.

* * *

What company hired Martina Navratilova to endorse their products?

Snap-On Tools.

* * *

Why does Martina Navratilova call her girl friend "Crème de Menthe?"

She's her favorite licker.

* * *

What nourishment sustains Martina Navratilova during a tennis tournament?

Box lunches.

When did the other tennis players suspect Martina Navratilova was a dyke?
When they saw her rolling her own tampons.

* * *

How does Martina Navratilova pick up another female tennis player?
She starts by complimenting her on a nice set.

* * *

When did the other tennis players suspect Martina Navratilova was gay?
When she came into the locker room and said she'd lick everyone in the place.

* * *

What did Martina Navratilova say to the other gay tennis player?
"Your face or mine?"

* * *

Why does Martina Navratilova love soybeans?
She's into meat substitutes.

* * *

What's endless love?
Stevie Wonder playing tennis with Ray Charles.

* * *

Why did the manufacturer recall all the John McEnroe tennis rackets?
Every time a player lost, they'd fly off the handle.

How can you tell if you're really cross-eyed?
    You can watch a tennis match without moving your head.

* * *

One tennis player ran into another at the club and asked, "How come Henry's not your doubles partner anymore?"
    The other player replied, "Would you partner with a guy who was always late, always tried to borrow money, blamed you viciously for every loss, and tried to screw both your wife and your teenage daughter?"
    "Of course I wouldn't."
    "Well, neither would Henry."

* * *

How do you know a lot of women tennis players are gay?
    When you walk into the locker room, you'll notice the stools are upside down.

* * *

What's worse than lobsters crawling on your tennis court?
    Crabs on your balls.

* * *

Why are so many female tennis players lesbians?
    After so many hours practicing every day, the last thing they want to do is play with balls.

* * *

How can you tell a female tennis player is gay?
    From the traces of K-Y jelly on her racket handle.

* * *

Why do lesbian tennis stars have such an easy time getting laid?
    Every tournament has a box office.

* * *

Why is a nymphomaniac movie star like a tennis player?
    They both like new balls for every set.

* * *

How do you tell a WASP widow?
    She's the one in the black tennis outfit.

Golf Jokes

An avid golfer is killed in an automobile accident, and moments later he finds himself at the pearly gates. St. Peter tells him he's been expected and he's free to walk right in. The golfer, though, has a question. "St. Peter, I'd like to know if there's a golf course in heaven."

"No, my son," the saint replies. "No course."

The golfer turns away, figuring he'll see what the situation is in hell. He arrives at the gates of hell and asks Satan, "You got a golf course here?"

The Prince of Darkness beams. "The best course ever created. Take a look for yourself."

The golfer walks in, follows directions, and arrives at the most beautiful 18 holes he's ever seen. Beaming, he turns to an imp in the pro shop and says, "My good man, get me some clubs and balls, and I'll be off."

"Sorry," the imp replies.

"What do you mean, sorry?" the golfer demands.

"We don't have a single club or ball in all of hell."

"Then how can I be expected to play?" the golfer asks.

The imp smiles. "That's the hell of it."

The tee-off time had been 7 AM, so the golfing fanatic's wife began to worry when he was late for dinner. She was almost ready to call the police when he pulled in the driveway a little after 6 PM.

"What happened?" she asked. "I was beside myself."

"Bill had a heart attack on the fifth tee," her husband replied.

"That's awful," she said. "You must be emotionally exhausted."

"That isn't the half of it," the husband replied. "It took me the whole day. Hit a shot, drag Bill, hit a shot, drag Bill..."

* * *

Why do nymphomaniacs like professional golfers?

Pro golfers love to get their balls close to the hole, then sink their one-foot putts.

* * *

The dumb kid goes to the golf course one morning looking for work and ends up being assigned to caddy for one of the members. The man says to the kid, "Come on, let's get my clubs out of my car."

The kid follows the man to his gleaming new Mercedes convertible. When the kid reaches in the trunk for the golf bag, a few golf tees fall out. "What are those things?" he asks.

The man replies, "Those are tees. I put my balls on them when I drive."

The kid opens his mouth in awe. "Golly, gee. Those Mercedes people think of everything!"

* * *

One man was sitting next to a friend at the country club.

"Bill, did I tell you I finally got old Higgins out for a round of golf?"

"No. How'd he do?"

"Not too good. He ruptured himself on the first tee. And it was my fault."

"Your fault? What happened?" Bill asked.

The first man replied, "Before I could explain, he saw the sign for the ball cleaner and . . ."

* * *

Did you hear about the two professional golfers who had a long argument about who was the bigger stud?

They decided to settle the argument by an 18-hole playoff.

* * *

What's the definition of a Ladies Professional Golf Association tournament?

Seventy-two holes playing 72 holes.

* * *

The guy had just teed up his ball on the first hole and was about to drive when a frantic girl in a bridal gown ran up to him and started pulling him toward the parking lot.

The guy listened for a moment, then shoved her away. "For Christ's sake, Jennifer!" he said. "I told you, only if it rains!"

* * *

The regular foursome was marching down the seventh fairway when they spotted a funeral procession traveling slowly down the road that ran along the side of the course. Watson, one of the members of the foursome, stopped, removed his hat, placed it over his heart, and stared at the ground for a moment in silent prayer.

One of his friends waited until he was through, then said, "Watson, old boy, that was a very nice gesture."

Watson shrugged. "It was the least I could do. We would have been married 41 years next month."

* * *

The avid golfer was sitting in the clubhouse having a drink after the game when a gorgeous blonde sat down next to him. They started chatting and really hit it off. Finally, the golfer invited the blonde to spend next weekend with him in Bermuda.

The blonde replied, "I'd love to. But before we get involved, there's something you should know about me. I'm a hooker."

The golfer patted her on the arm. "That's okay. We'll just change your stance and grip a little and you'll be all right."

* * *

"My husband makes love like an artist," the woman bragged. "Gentle stroke after stroke after stroke, for hours, until I'm trembling with passion."

Her friend grunted. "You're lucky. In bed, my husband's a golfer."

'A golfer?''

"Yeah. He wants to get into the hole in as few strokes as possible."

* * *

How can you tell a golfer is an incorrigible cheater?

When he makes a hole in one, he puts "0" on the scorecard.

* * *

The golfer met an old friend he hadn't seen recently at the bar in the clubhouse. They chatted for a while until the friend said, "I saw you and your wife tee off in the couples tournament yesterday. I was happy to see you finally got her out of that terrible stance she used to use."

The golfer shook his head. "That wasn't a new stance. I went out and got a new wife."

* * *

How can you tell a guy's a really lousy golfer?

He loses his ball in the washer on the first tee.

* * *

The businessman dropped dead on the third hole of the golf course, and it fell to his playing partner to break the news to his widow. He spent a while thinking of a gentle way to tell her. Finally, he dialed and said, "Agnes, this is Fred. I'm afraid I've got some bad news for you. Bill lost $10,000 playing golf this morning."

"That bum!" Agnes exclaimed. "He should drop dead from shame."

Fred said, "Now that you mentioned it . . ."

* * *

Why did the golfer's wife divorce him?

She discovered he'd been making a lot of five-footers on the course.

* * *

And then there was the woman who won the competition between members of every country club in the county.

The speaker introduced her as the "intercourse champion of Fairfield County."

The prime minister of Israel was in Italy on a state visit, so he called the Vatican and asked the pope if he'd join him in a golf game. Well, there aren't many golf courses in Poland, so John Paul didn't have the first idea what the game was about. Finally, after meeting with his advisers, he decided to call Jack Nicklaus and plead with him to take his place. When Nicklaus agreed, Pope John Paul called the prime minister and told him he was too sick to play golf. To cover the deception, His Holiness made Nicklaus an official member of the College of Cardinals and sent him in his place.

All day the pope waited for Nicklaus to return to the Vatican. When he did, the pope asked, "How badly did you beat him?"

"I lost," Nicklaus replied.

"Wow," the Pope exclaimed, "the prime minister must be some golfer."

"He called in sick," Nicklaus said. "I lost to Rabbi Palmer."

* * *

Why is golf like a penis?

The more you play, the harder it gets.

* * *

Jesus, Moses, and an old man come to the tee of a par-three hole. Moses tees off first but slices the ball into a huge pond. Calmly, he walks over to the pond, waves his club, parts the water, then chips the ball up onto the green.

Jesus has the honor next, and he slices the ball into the water, too. He walks over to the pond, walks across the top of the water, takes a mightly swing with a wedge, and lofts the ball onto the green.

The old man hits last. His ball heads straight for the water, but as it hits the surface, a fish jumps up and swallows it. The fish is then immediately grabbed by a hawk, which flys up, then dumps the fish on the green. The fish spits out the ball, which rolls into the cup.

Jesus says to the old man, "Nice shot, Dad, but would you quit fucking around and play golf?"

* * *

Why did God invent golf?

So white people could dress up like black people.

* * *

How can you tell if a golfer is nearsighted?

He's driving his caddy's nuts.

* * *

What's the difference between a golf course and a woman?

A woman's hole is in the middle of the rough.

* * *

What happens if a lady golfer suffers a cut between the first and second hole?

The space is so small, it's hard to use a Band-Aid.

* * *

Why did the gynecologist give the lady golfer twelve tampons?

That was par for her hole.

Hockey Jokes

How do you prevent a hockey player from charging?
  Take away his credit card.

* * *

How did the hockey player break his finger?
  Someone punched him in the nose.

* * *

What's the difference between baseball groupies and hockey groupies?
  Baseball groupies don't have hair on their chests.

* * *

What do you call five hockey players around the face-off circle?
  A dope ring.

* * *

Two explorers were lost deep in the heart of Africa when they wandered into a cannibal village. They were nervous, but it soon appeared that the natives had more than enough food. Having starved for weeks, the explorers finally were desperate enough to go into the cannibal butcher shop. When they walked in, the cannibal who owned the store said, "You guys are lucky. We got a special on brains this week. We got some missionary brains at $3.50 a pound. Some diplomat brains at $4.50 a pound. Over there are some movie star brains at $6.00 a pound."

The explorers were a trifle repulsed. But they knew they had to eat. One pointed to a corner of the store. "What are those over there?"

The cannibal replied, "Those are hockey player brains. $500 a pound."

"Five hundred dollars!" one explorer exclaimed. "They must be delicious."

"That's not it," the cannibal replied. "Do you know how many hockey players you have to kill to get a pound of brains?"

* * *

Why is a Harlem crack dealer like a hockey player's agent?
  They're both dope peddlers.

* * *

Why did they ban "the wave" from hockey stadiums?
  Too many fans were drowning.

* * *

Why did the National Hockey League draft Indira Gandhi?
  She stopped seven shots in four seconds.

* * *

What's a formal hockey banquet?

All the players arrive with their flies zipped.

* * *

The college hockey star was stopped on the way to the rink by a coed. "I've got to talk with you, Brian," she said.

"I can't talk now," he said. "I'll be in trouble if I miss the first period."

"You're already in trouble," she said. "I missed my first period."

* * *

Did you hear about the hockey coach who was fired because of illness and fatigue?

The owner was sick and tired of the way the team played.

* * *

Why have hockey players started to wear helmets?

So they know which end to wipe.

* * *

Why did the visiting hockey player have such a horrible hangover the first morning in Toronto?

At the airport, he saw a big sign that said, "Drink Canada Dry," so he went out that night and tried.

* * *

Why don't hockey players ever clean out their ears?

Their heads would cave in.

* * *

How did the Polish hockey team drown?
  Spring training.

* * *

Why did the entire hockey team have bad body odor on one side?
  They couldn't find any Left Guard.

* * *

Why did they call timeout in the leper hockey game?
  There was a face off in the corner.

* * *

Why did the hockey player wear a big CASH ONLY sign around his neck?
  To keep the opposing players from giving him a check.

* * *

Why has the U.S. hockey team lost so many games since Reagan's been in office?
  The president's refused to let the team play a left wing.

* * *

Why don't hockey players mind if girls have their periods?
  Hockey players are used to crossing the red line.

* * *

How can you tell a hockey player's birthday cake?
  No icing.

* * *

Why are hockey players such lousy lovers?
  It usually takes them twenty shots on goal before they score.

* * *

Why is a hockey player like a hockey groupie?
  They both change their pads after every three periods.

* * *

Did you hear about the member of Canada's Parliament who gave a stirring speech against pornographic video tapes?
  He was referring to hockey highlight films.

* * *

What's the difference between the *Friday the 13th* films and a hockey game?
  A *Friday the 13th* film has less slashing.

* * *

What's the difference between a hockey player and a pit bull terrier?
  Skates.

* * *

  The hooker was sitting at the bar next to an extremely morose man. She finally said, "What's the problem, pal?"
  "I'm a hockey goalie," the guy said. "Tonight, I had such a bad period, my coach fined me a day's pay."
  "You think you got troubles?" the hooker said. "When I have a bad period, I lose a week's pay."

Boxing Jokes

What's the difference between Marvin Hagler and a one-inch cock?
  You wouldn't want to fuck with either one of them.

* * *

Why are boxers so hardheaded?
  Their skulls protect the weakest part of their bodies.

* * *

What do a boxer's brain and a zucchini have in common?
  They're both types of squash.

* * *

The boxer was brought in as an opponent for the champ in a tuneup bout. Reporters suspected the guy had been in far too many fights, but the promoter assured them he was a legitimate opponent. Finally, under pressure, the promoter arranged a press conference for the big heavyweight.

The first question from a reporter was, "What do you think of Las Vegas?"

The boxer replied, "He's a jerk. I knocked him out in da first round."

* * *

The heavyweight was getting creamed in the fight, but every round he managed to stagger back to the corner. At the end of the eighth round, he could barely see from the blood streaming down his forehead. His manager said to him, "Hold on just a couple rounds. I think you're going to win."

"Win," the pug grunted. "I can't even see to hit him."

"I know," the manager replied. "But the sight of you is beginning to make him sick."

* * *

Why wasn't John F. Kennedy a good boxer?
He couldn't take a shot to the head.

* * *

What's the best way to get an Irish boxer to take a dive?
Pour whiskey on the canvas.

* * *

Who's the most respected man in all of sports?
Heavyweight champion Mike Tyson — everyone he's fought has ended up looking up to him.

* * *

How can you tell a guy is a lousy boxer?

He sells advertising space on the soles of his shoes.

* * *

The Puerto Rican guy's dream was having a son who would grow up to be a world champion boxer. After two daughters, his wife finally delivered a son. The doctor asked him what the baby boy's name would be.

"Anita," the Puerto Rican replied.

"Juan, you're crazy!" his wife exclaimed. "Why would you give him a girl's name?"

The Puerto Rican said, "With a name like Anita, he'll learn to fight like a champ by the time he's five."

* * *

Three boxing managers met at the gym. The first manager bragged, "My number-one boy just won the world bantamweight championship."

The second manager said, "That's great. But I'm almost there, too. My pug's the number-one lightweight contender." He turned to the third manager and asked, "Jake, how's your heavyweight doing?"

Jake said, "He's a crossword-puzzle fighter."

"What's a crossword-puzzle fighter?"

Jake sighed. "He enters the ring vertical and leaves horizontal."

* * *

The heavyweight champ was out on the town with his girlfriend when he was accosted in an alley by a mugger that couldn't have weighed more than 110 pounds. The girlfriend was astounded when the champ meekly handed over his wallet. When the mugger fled, she demanded, "I don't understand. Why didn't you knock that guy through the wall?''

The champ looked peeved. ''Hey, I only had a few grand in my wallet. I never fight for less than a million.''

* * *

The pug's face looked like it had been through a meat grinder, but that didn't stop him from bragging nonstop at the bar. Finally, one guy said, ''Why don't you just shut up, you bum.''

The pug said indignantly, ''I'm no bum. Why I once sent Mohammed Ali to the floor.''

''I don't believe it,'' the guy replied.

''He's right,'' the bartender said. ''I saw the fight.''

The guy started to apologize to the fighter when the bartender continued, ''Ali tripped over this chump's body in the middle of the ring.''

* * *

A guy walked into a bar that was a hangout for professional athletes. The place was pretty empty. He was on his second drink when he spotted a tall, rugged-looking guy sitting morosely in the corner, crying into his beer. The guy gestured to the bartender and asked, ''What's with that guy over there?''

The bartender said, ''He's had three no-hitters in a row.''

The guy exclaimed, ''Then why isn't he celebrating?''

''Because he's a boxer,'' the bartender replied.

* * *

What's the definition of ''dumb''?

A boxer who rolls up his sleeve when a girl says she wants to feel his muscle.

* * *

Why is a lousy prize fighter like a baby?
    They both get a bust in the mouth.

* * *

What do you call a huge white heavyweight beating the shit
out of a punch-drunk black fighter?
    A fair fight.

* * *

Why did the post office decide not to issue a stamp honoring
the heavyweight champion of the world?
    Nobody could lick it.

* * *

Why is heavyweight Mike Tyson like a blow job?
    It's hard to beat either one.

* * *

Why is a boxer's cup like a millionaire's wall safe?
    They're both designed to protect the family jewels.

* * *

What's the definition of "gibberish"?
    A conversation between Joe Louis and Mohammed Ali.

* * *

What happens to the world's sleaziest con men?
    They all head international boxing federations.

* * *

What's the significance of the number 66?
 It's the sum of the IQs of the U.S. Olympic boxing team.

* * *

What happened to the boxer who broke his left hand?
 He's all right.

* * *

Jokes About Other Sports

The young guy from Detroit was on his way to stardom on the pro bowling tour, but he had very little experience with women. Finally, a woman he met at a publicity party wangled an invitation back to his hotel room. Unfortunately, the young man had no idea what to do.

Finally, the woman said, "Listen. All you have to do is take the hardest thing you got and put it where women pee."

So the guy got his bowling ball and dropped it in the sink.

* * *

The busy executive's wife was moaning about all the time she had on her hands. So he said to her, "Listen, what you need is a hobby. Why don't you take up some sport, like golf. Here's a couple hundred dollars for lessons."

He forgot about the conversation shortly. But he assumed that she'd taken his advice, because she seemed happier. A couple of weeks later, he came home and overheard his wife saying on the phone, "I finally got through a game without losing a ball. And my score was 38."

The executive was astounded. When his wife got off the phone, he kissed her and said, "Honey, I underestimated your athletic ability. After only two weeks, you played nine holes of golf in 38 strokes and didn't lose a ball."

The wife looked at him as if he were crazy. "I didn't take up golf," she said. "I was talking about my bowling."

* * *

Just before dinner one night, this guy's wife discovers she's out of milk, so she sends him down to 7-Eleven for a half gallon. On the way back, he spots his favorite local tavern, so he decides to stop in for a quick shot. When he walks in the door, two friends are sitting at the bar, and they both buy him a shot and a beer. An hour later, he's still sitting at the bar.

His friends leave, and he's about to go home to face the music when a gorgeous cashier from the supermarket walks into the bar and sits next to him. She starts openly flirting, and after two drinks her hands are all over him. They leave and go back to her apartment, where she gives him the night of his life.

Finally, as the sun peeps above the horizon, the guy gets dressed. Before he leaves, he asks the girl, "Do you have any baby powder?" She directs him to the medicine cabinet, where he finds a bottle that he uses to dust his hands. Then he stumbles out to his car and drives home.

His wife is waiting at the door, ready to kill. "What in the hell have you been up to?" she demands.

"It's this way," the guy said. "I stopped into Gleason's for a pop, and a couple guys bought me a few rounds. Then Jenny, the cashier from the supermarket, came in and started to flirt. Next thing I remember, we were back at her apartment getting naked and...."

"Yeah, sure," the wife said. "Give me your hands."

The guy stuck his hands out. She inspected them, then screamed, "I knew it — you've been bowling again!"

* * *

A Polack moved to a small town in Alabama and he asked the locals what they did for fun.

"We go to town and beat up Niggers," they said. The Polack decided to join them the next Friday night. The pack of rednecks wandered into the gas station and the pool hall without finding a victim, but to their delight, a whole crowd of blacks were in the bowling alley. The rednecks whooped, charged, and began beating up the blacks.

Anxious to be one of the boys, the Polack took a crowbar and started smashing the bowling balls. "What the fuck are you doing?" one of the rednecks shouted.

"You get the big ones," the Polack replied, "I'll take care of the eggs."

* * *

Why would women rather screw than bowl?

The balls are lighter and you don't have to change your shoes.

* * *

How can you recognize a chic Polish woman?

She'll be wearing open-toed bowling shoes.

* * *

Why do librarians make lousy bowlers?

They hate noise so much they can't stand to hear a pin drop.

Why are dirty old men such lousy bowlers?
  Their minds are in the gutter.

* * *

Why did the nymphomaniac go to the bowling hall?
  She wanted a few strikes up her alley.

* * *

What's the difference between your wife and your bowling ball?
  You can only fit three fingers in your bowling ball.

* * *

What do you get when you cross Howard Cosell and a prostitute?
  A fucking know-it-all.

* * *

When is Howard Cosell bullshitting?
  When his lips are moving.

* * *

How can you identify a Polack at the horse races?
  He's the one entering a mule.

* * *

How can you recognize a Jew at the race track?
  He bets on the mule.

* * *

How can you tell an Italian is at the race track?
 The mule wins.

* * *

Why did the cheerleader snort NutraSweet?
 She thought it was Diet Coke.

* * *

Two guys were sitting at a bar and struck up a conversation. One asked the other, "So what do you do for a living?"
 The second guy replied, "Well, I used to be a professional wrestler."
 The first guy glanced at the second guy's decidedly scrawny body and said, "I can't believe it."
 "Not only that, I won my first ten matches."
 "So why did you quit?" the first guy asked.
 The second guy replied, "For my eleventh match, they made me fight a man."

* * *

Why are so many blacks such great sprinters?
 Their coaches tell them if they don't win the race, they'll have to take a bath.

* * *

One kid said to another, "Hey, my brother runs the 100 in ten flat."
 "That's nothing," the other kid said. "My brother does it in five seconds."
 "That's impossible."
 "Oh, yeah?" the kid said. "My brother knows a shortcut."

* * *

Why did the coach of the women's track team only recruit black girls who were virgins?
   If they hadn't been screwed, they could run faster than their brothers.

* * *

Why are most sports team owners "ethnosexuals?"
   They love to fuck blacks and Puerto Ricans.

* * *

Why won't they allow any blacks to try out for the U.S. Olympic swimming team?
   They leave rings around the pool.

* * *

Why is a female gymnast like a nymphomaniac?
   They both excel in floor exercises.

* * *

How can you tell if a female gymnast is really agile?
   She can pull out her own tampon with her teeth.

* * *

How can you tell if a female gymnast is still a virgin?
   If her male coach is still working hard on her vault.

* * *

What's sex?
   Poor man's polo.

* * *

Why aren't there any black championship cross-country skiers?
The watermelons in their backpacks slow them down.

* * *

Why do so many black runners train with their Walkmans on?
The tape plays, "Left, right, left, right, left, right..."

* * *

Why don't Polacks water-ski?
They've never found a lake on a hill.

* * *

When will the Olympics be held in China?
When laundry becomes an Olympic event.

* * *

Why does the Russian women's track team wear sleeveless jerseys?
They like the feeling of the wind through their hair.

* * *

Why did the Polish skier show up with only one ski?
The forecast was for one foot of snow.

* * *

Why did the Russian woman sprinter miss the Olympic games?
She cut her toes shaving.

* * *

How does the news report of a World Cup soccer match usually read?

"Among those wounded in the riot were..."

* * *

Why are Innuit hookers like sports agents?

They're both good at snow jobs.

* * *

Why do so few Polacks play professional sports?

They can't get their names on the back of a uniform.

* * *

Did you hear about the Polish terrorists?

They attacked the Special Olympics.

* * *

The gun went off and eight women dived into the pool for the first heat of the Olympic 100-meter breaststroke. An American won in a little under two minutes, six women finished within ten seconds of her—and the Polish contestant finished thirty-five minutes later.

When she jumped out of the pool, she ran over to the judges and screamed, "I protest. Those other girls cheated."

"How did they cheat?" a judge asked.

The Polish swimmer replied, "They used their arms."

* * *

Why are sports agents such good laxatives?

Because they irritate the shit out of everybody.

* * *

Why do black athletes have such foul mouths?
 You ever see a black home with soap?

* * *

Why did the Mafia godfather list his profession as ''sports mechanic?''
 He made his living fixing ball games.

* * *

The first round World Cup soccer match between Italy and Poland turned increasingly violent as fight after fight marked the play. Finally, after four Italian subs had rushed onto the field in the middle of play to slug a Pole, the referees banished the entire Italian team to the locker room.
 Twenty minutes later, the Polish team scored a goal.

* * *

What's a race track?
 A place where windows clean people.

* * *

What's horse sense?
 What a horse has that keeps him from betting on people.

* * *

What's a racehorse?
 An animal that can take several thousand horse players for a ride at the same time.

* * *

The millionaire sportsman was showing a new friend

around his mansion. In every room were the trophies of his hunts — lions, tigers, elephants, and other rare animals. Finally, he led the friend into a special room where spotlights shone down on a mountain lion.

"Why the special treatment for an ordinary mountain lion?" the friend asked.

"Appearances can be deceiving," the millionaire replied. "It's the way this lion was stuffed that makes him special."

"What's he stuffed with?"

"My wife," the millionaire replied.

* * *

The new coach of the woman's softball team asked the coed what her best position was.

She immediately stripped naked, then got down on her hands and knees.

* * *

The guy in the flashy leisure suit looked very out of place in the clubhouse of the Kentucky race track. As one blue-blood watched, the guy went up to the window to bet, placed $50,000 to win on the number 4 horse. Five minutes later, the guy went back to bet another $50,000. A few minutes later, he stood up with an even bigger wad in his hand. The Kentucky horseman felt a pang of compassion and stopped the guy, saying, "You're not going to bet on Number 4 again, are you?"

"So what if I am?" the guy said in a thick New York accent.

"Number 4 has absolutely no chance to win. He doesn't have any speed. I know, because I own him."

"Maybe so," the New Yorker said, "but it's gonna be a damn slow race. You see, I own the other four horses."

* * *

What's the difference between a chess player and your wife in bed?

Every once in a while, a chess player moves.

* * *

What's the difference between circus midgets and a women's track team?

One's a bunch of cunning runts and...

* * *

Why did the women's softball coach tattoo his players' names on their thighs?

So he could find his way to the right batter's box.

* * *

Why are there so many great black hurdlers?

They grow up jumping subway turnstiles.

* * *

Why are there so many great black high jumpers?

That's how they get into pay toilets.

* * *

The athletes scheduled to compete in an international track meet were on a plane flying over the Atlantic. Suddenly, the plane developed engine trouble. The pilot announced, "I'm afraid we're all going to die if three of you passengers don't volunteer to jump to save the rest."

There was silence for a moment. Then a French sprinter got up, went to the door, shouted, "Vive la France!" and jumped out of the plane.

A few minutes later, a British pole vaulter got up, went to

the door, shouted, "God save the Queen!" and jumped into the sea.

A few minutes later, a burly Texas shotputter got up, went to the door, shouted "Remember the Alamo!" and tossed a Mexican runner out of the plane.

* * *

What's wrong with the brand new soccer stadium in Warsaw?
    Everywhere you sit, you're behind a Pole.

* * *

Why hasn't Puerto Rico won more Olympic gold medals?
    Because car-stripping isn't an Olympic event.

* * *

The skipper of the America's Cup yacht strolled into an Australian whorehouse to relieve some of the tension from competition. He selected a well-stacked young lady, took her upstairs, and climbed aboard. About fifteen minutes later, the yachtsman grunted, "How am I doing?"
    The hooker replied, "Three knots."
    The skipper said, "What do you mean, three knots?"
    "You're not in, you're not hard, and you're not getting your money back."

* * *

What do hookers call jockeys?
    Low blows.

* * *

How come most professional wrestlers are bastards?
    Because their mothers were pinned more often than they were.

What do you call a homosexual's athletic supporter?
A fruit cup.

* * *

Why do racehorses have four feet?
Because six inches isn't long enough.

* * *

Why have no lepers ever made an Olympic relay team?
They always lose their legs.

* * *

What goes "Huff, thud, huff, thud, huff, squish, shish?"
A jogger stepping in dogshit.

* * *

Why do college athletes read *Playboy*?
It improves hand-eye co-ordination.

* * *

Why are there so few good black gymnasts?
When they're tumbling, their lips stick to the floor mat.

* * *

Why didn't the Mexicans enter a team in the 1984 Olympic Games?
Everyone in Mexico who can run, jump, or swim is already in the U.S.

* * *

Why aren't there any good Polish race-car drivers?
  They always open the door to let out the clutch.

* * *

Why aren't there any leper high divers?
  They keep losing their nerves.

* * *

Why do male runners have much faster times than female runners?
  Male runners have two ball bearings and a stick shift.

* * *

Why haven't any Polish drivers won the Indianapolis 500?
  They have to stop ten times to ask directions.

* * *

Why hasn't the yacht from Haiti ever won an America's Cup race?
  It's hard to sail with 937 people on board.

* * *

Why do Puerto Rican runners never win at indoor track meets?
  They always stop to spray-paint the walls.

* * *

Why do women like hunters?
  They go deep into the bush, they always shoot twice, and they always eat what they shoot.

Why aren't there any black race-car drivers?
Race cars don't have whitewalls and power windows.

* * *

The two Polish hunters were driving into the woods when they saw a sign that said BEAR LEFT.
So they went home.

* * *

Two Polish hunters prepared for weeks for their hunting trip. They gathered guns, ammunition, clothing, hats, boots, supplies, and the services of three of the finest hunting dogs they could find. But every single day, after twelve hours in the woods, they'd come out empty-handed while other hunters staggered under a load of dead pheasants, quail, ducks, and geese.

One of the hunters finally said to the other, "What are we doing wrong? We spent a fortune preparing for this trip."

"I can't think of a thing," the other hunter said. "Except maybe we're not throwing the dogs high enough."

* * *

Two city slickers went hunting once a year. Finally, their luck ran out and one shot the other after mistaking him for a deer. The one guy carried his friend out of the woods to the car, then drove him to the hospital emergency room.

After his friend had been examined, the first guy asked the doctor, "Is Bill going to make it?"

"I don't know," the doctor replied. "He'd have a better chance if you hadn't gutted him and tied him to the hood of your car."

* * *

Why don't Polacks hunt elephants?
  They get tired of carrying the wooden decoys.

* * *

What's a queer sports agent?
  A guy who likes girls more than money.

* * *

What's the shortest book in the world?
  Negroes I Have Met While Yachting.

* * *

Why do women have cunts?
  So athletes will talk to them.

* * *

How can you tell if a track star is gay?
  He's always letting the other runners lap him.

* * *

Why is it that young black males are either track stars or rapists?
  Both involve sprinting and broad-jumping.

* * *

Why did they install TV sets in Polish stadiums?
  So the fans could see what was going on in their local bar.

* * *

Why are Puerto Ricans banned from the Indianapolis 500?
  Every time a car makes a pit stop, they strip it.

Why did the Polish skier freeze to death?
He tried to take his pants off over his skis.

* * *

What's the difference between Teddy Ruxpin and a Russian female track star?
Teddy Ruxpin has less fur in his armpits.

* * *

Why did the black sprinter get blown before every race?
He loved a head start.

* * *

What happened to the Polish water polo team?
The horses drowned.

* * *

Did you hear about the Polish athlete who won an Olympic gold medal?
He had it bronzed.

* * *

Two Polish guys rented a rowboat to go fishing. For once in their lives, they had great luck, pulling in at least a couple of dozen fish. Finally, as the sun was setting, one Polack said to the other, "Hey, we gotta go. We'll come back tomorrow."

"How are we going to find this spot?" his friend asked.

"Easy," the first guy said. He took out a pencil and drew a big X on the bottom of the boat.

The other guy shook his head. "Now, that's stupid."

"What do you mean, stupid?"

"What if we don't get the same boat?"

Every year, the woods were overpopulated by more inexperienced hunters from the city. So the old woodsman finally had his wife sew him an outfit of wild black-and-white stripes. "No one's going to mistake me for a deer," he said. Then he left for the woods.

Two hours later, his wife got a call to rush to the hospital, where her husband lay critically wounded from a gunshot. In the waiting room, she discovered a distraught stockbroker from Manhattan who'd shot him.

"How could you?" she screamed. "How could you possibly mistake my husband for a deer?"

"Who said anything about a deer?" the city slicker replied. "I thought he was a zebra."

* * *

A hunter was deep in the marshes hunting ducks. He sat still in his blind for hours and hours. Finally, he got his shot as a duck flew far overhead. The hunter sighted, fired, then, to his great delight, the duck plummetted to earth.

The hunter took off at great speed to claim his trophy. When he got to the spot, he found a local backwoodsman staring at the bird. The hunter bragged to him, "Bet you never saw a shot like that, did you?"

The backwoodsman shrugged, spit tobacco, then remarked, "You wasted a bullet. From that height, the fall alone would have killed him."

* * *

Did you hear about the new glass-bottomed boats?

Now the fish can brag about how big the guy was they got away from.

* * *

The man spent the best part of the day in the local tavern,

but around sunset he staggered out and made his way to the fish store. He stood in the doorway and yelled to the owner, "Hey, Jack, toss me four trout."

Jack said, "Why can't I just put them in a bag for you?"

The man replied, "My wife thinks I was fishing. I want to be able to tell her I caught four trout."

* * *

Dolores's husband was a notorious man about town, and she'd given him warning that his next transgression would be his last. One night her best friend saw the husband staggering home in the wee hours of the morning. But to the friend's surprise, there was no explosion. The next day she asked Dolores, "What happened last night? I thought you were going to throw that bum out the next time he was out on the town?"

Dolores said, "He told me he'd been fishing."

"But he didn't have any fish."

Dolores replied, "That's why I believed him."

* * *

The man was showing home videos of his latest vacation to a group of bored relatives. His narration led up to the highlight of the trip, a deep-sea fishing voyage. The film showed him arriving at the dock with his catch. He explained, "Here I am coming back home with a world-record marlin."

His brother-in-law scoffed, "You've got to be kidding. That fish you're holding can't be more than a foot long."

"Well," the man explained, "in a half day of fighting, a fish can lose a lot of weight."

* * *

Three Polacks had just put their lines in the water when the game warden appeared. One guy immediately threw down his rod and began running into the woods as fast as he could. The game warden gave chase for nearly twenty minutes before he brought the guy down with a flying tackle.

"All right," the warden said, "show me some I.D."

The Polack pulled out his wallet and produced some papers. The game warden looked at them, then said to the Polack in amazement, "I don't understand why you were running. It's the first day of trout season and you've got a valid fishing license."

"I know," the Polack said. "But my friends don't."

* * *

Three Polacks went hunting one day. After a few hours with no luck, they decided to split up. One Polack asked his friends, "What do we do if we get lost?"

"Just fire three shots into the air and we'll find you," the second said.

They separated. A couple of hours later, the first Polack knew he was lost. He fired one shot, then a second, then a third. But no one came to his rescue. "Oh no!" he exclaimed to himself. "No one's saving me — and I'm almost out of arrows."

* * *

A man had been out fishing all day long, and he'd tried every lure he owned. But after seven hours, he hadn't had a nibble. Disgusted, he pulled out his wallet, took out some bills, and tossed them into the water. "There!" he yelled to the fish. "Go buy something you do like."

* * *

Why do marathon runners eat refried beans?

To get a second wind.

How can you tell if a water polo team is gay?
The pool is full of blowfish.